NORTH AMERICAN MAMMALS
Caribou

Jinny Johnson

Published by Smart Apple Media,
an imprint of Black Rabbit Books
P.O. Box 3263, Mankato, Minnesota, 56002
www.blackrabbitbooks.com

Printed in the United States of America,
at Corporate Graphics in North Mankato, Minnesota.

Designed by Hel James
Edited by Mary-Jane Wilkins

Cataloging-in-Publication Data
is available from the Library of Congress

ISBN 978-1-62588-033-8

Photo acknowledgements
t = top, b = bottom
title page Sergey Krasnoshchokov/Shutterstock;
page 3 Stockphoto/Thinkstock; 4 Louise Cukrov/Shutterstock;
7 Stockphoto/Thinkstock; 8 Paul Nicklen, 9 Marc Lester/
both Getty Images; 10 Jupiterimages/Thinkstock;
11t Gucio_55/Shutterstock; 12 Sergey Krasnoshchokov/
Shutterstock; 13t F1online/Thinkstock; 14 miker, 15 Rustam
R. Fazlaev/both Shutterstock; 16 Medioimages/Photodisc,
17 Purestock/both Thinkstock; 18 Hemera Technologies,
19 Comstock/both Thinkstock; 21 iStockphoto/Thinkstock;
22t Vladimir Melnikov, b lantapix/both Shutterstock;
23 Sergey Krasnoshcho}kov/Shutterstock
Cover Randy Yarbrough/Shutterstock

DAD0509
052013
1 2 3 4 5 6 7 8 9

Contents

I'm a caribou.

My home is in the far north of North America.

3

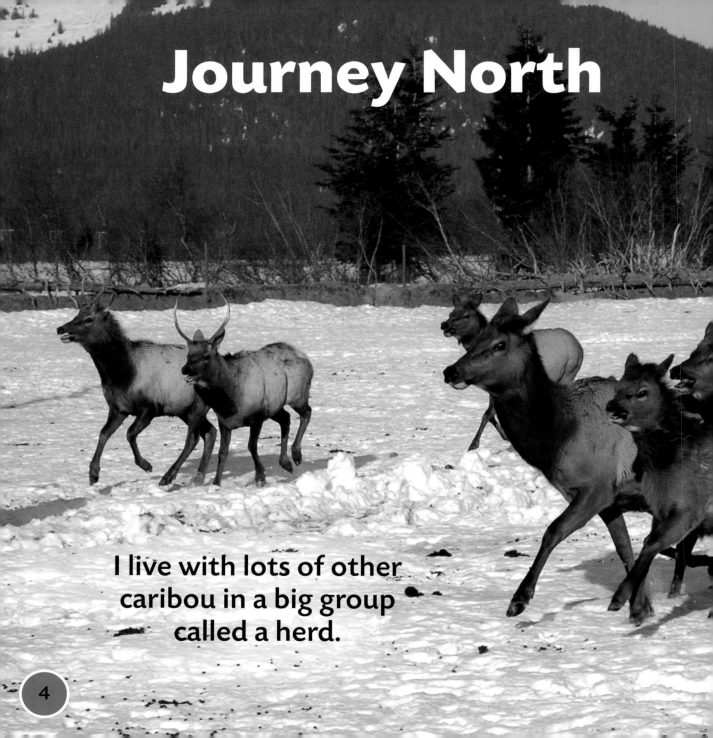

Journey North

I live with lots of other caribou in a big group called a herd.

Each spring we leave the forests where we spend the winter and begin a long journey north.

We travel hundreds of miles to the Arctic tundra. This is where we live in the summer and where we give birth to our young.

Summer Home

Why do we make this long journey every year?

During the short tundra summer there is lots and lots of lovely fresh grass for us to eat. So it's the perfect place for our young calves to feed and grow.

But in winter the tundra is too cold for us, so we travel back to the forests.

Young Caribou

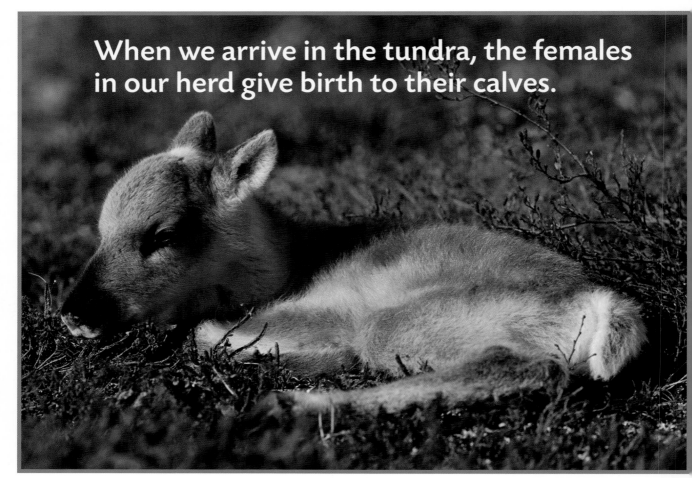

When we arrive in the tundra, the females in our herd give birth to their calves.

The calves are up on their feet almost right away. A calf can follow its mom around an hour after it is born.

The next day they can run faster than a human. Calves feed on their mother's milk for the first weeks, but soon they start to eat plants too.

Finding Food

Once the calves are born we can all get busy eating plenty of food.

We need to eat a lot in the summer because there is less food around for us in winter.

Grasses and other small plants are our favorites. In winter we eat anything we can find, but mostly lichen.

Fur and Feet

It's cold where we live, but we have a double coat of fur to keep us warm.

There's a thick wooly layer underneath and stiffer hairs on top to keep in the heat.

Our long legs help us run fast and our hooves are large and almost round. These act like snowshoes to stop us from sinking into snow or soft mud.

My Nose

Smell is my most important sense and I use my nose to help me find food.

I can even smell something tasty hidden under the snow. I can sniff out danger too —such as a nearby bear. If I'm scared, I release a smell from a place on my ankles. This warns other caribou to watch out.

Antlers

All full-grown caribou have antlers, but males have much bigger ones than females.

At the start of the mating season in fall, we males use our antlers in fierce battles over females. We lock antlers and wrestle until one of us is hurt or gives up.

After these battles, we lose our antlers. They grow again over the next year. Females usually keep their antlers through the winter and lose them in spring.

On the Move

We generally travel about 30 miles (48 km) a day when we're on the move.

We can move faster when we need to. I can run at up to 48 miles an hour (80 km/h) if I am being chased by a hungry wolf.

I'm happy in the water and can swim across rivers and lakes.

Journey South

In fall, we start the trek back south before our tundra home gets too cold and snowy. By then the calves are big and strong enough to travel with us.

We all stay together in a big herd. That means there are plenty of us to watch out for predators such as bears and wolves.

Caribou Facts

Caribou also live in northern Europe and Asia. In Europe they are known as reindeer.

A full-grown male caribou is about 6 feet (1.8 m) long and weighs about 242 pounds (110 kg). Females are slightly smaller. A male's antlers can grow 1 inch (2.5 cm) a day and weigh up to 33 pounds (15 kg).

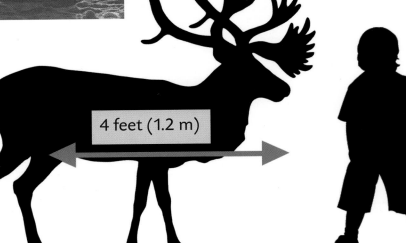

4 feet (1.2 m)

4 feet (1.2 m); height of average 7-year-old

Twice a year caribou make one of the longest journeys of any land animal when they move between the northern forests and the tundra.

Useful Words

antler A bony growth on the head of deer such as caribou.

Arctic tundra An area inside the Arctic Circle where there are no trees, but lots of plants grow in the short summer.

lichen A living thing that is part fungus and part plant.

Index

Web Link

Learn more about caribou at: http://kids.nationalgeographic.com/kids/animals/creaturefeature/caribou/